S/05

W9-CKH-946

ANIMALS
ANIMALS

BATS

BY MARGARET DORNFELD

BENCHMARK BOOKS

MARSHALL CAVENDISH
NEW YORK

Series Consultant
James Doherty
General Curator
Bronx Zoo, New York

Benchmark Books
Marshall Cavendish
99 White Plains Road
Tarrytown, NY 10591–9001
www.marshallcavendish.com

Library of Congress Cataloging–in–Publication Data

Dornfeld, Margaret.
Bats / Margaret Dornfeld.
p. cm. – (Animals, animals)
Includes bibliographical references and index.
ISBN 0–7614–1754–0
1. Bats–Juvenile literature. I. Title. II. Series.

QL737.C5D67 2004
599.4–dc22
2004009342

Photo research by Joan Meisel

Cover photo: Royalty–Free/Corbis

Photographs in this book are used by permission and through the courtesy of: *Bat Conservation International*: Mark and Selena Kiser, 37;
Elaine Acker, 40. *Corbis*: Eric and David Hosking, 4; Joe McDonald, 21, 32. *Peter Arnold, Inc.*: Gerard Lacz, 8; Gunter Ziesler, 14, 16, 19
(center); Michael Sewell, 19 (top); Eichaker/BIOS, 19 (bottom); Martin Harvey, 20; Fred Bruemmer, 22–23, 31; Albert Visage, 26, 38–39;
Roland Seitre, 34. *Photo Researchers, Inc.*: B. G. Thomson, 18 (top), 36; Larry L. Miller, 18 (bottom); Dr. Merlin Tuttle/BCI, 24, 28–29.

Printed in China
1 3 5 6 4 2

CONTENTS

1   INTRODUCING BATS 5

2   BAT BASICS 9

3   CALLING ALL BATS 17

4   LIVING UPSIDE DOWN 27

5   BATS AT RISK 35

GLOSSARY 42

FIND OUT MORE 44

INDEX 46

1
INTRODUCING BATS

A little brown bat wakes up in the evening. As night falls, it stretches its wings and flies off to feed. The bat snaps up bugs in the dark until its belly is full. Before morning, it returns to its home in an attic. It hangs upside down by its toes and falls asleep for the day.

For the little brown bat, this life is ordinary. But to people, it may seem a bit strange. Bats are often seen as spooky or mysterious. After all, they appear in the dark–ness and disappear with the dawn. Take a close look at a bat and it may seem even stranger. Many bats look like tiny goblins, with odd faces and oversized ears.

People have often tried to explain bats by letting their imaginations run wild. In Europe, people once thought bats were evil spirits or the souls of the dead.

THE GREATER HORSESHOE BAT LEAVES ITS HOME ABOUT AN HOUR AFTER SUNSET. IT SPENDS THE DAY HANGING UPSIDE DOWN UNDER THE ROOF OF A BUILDING OR A CAVE.

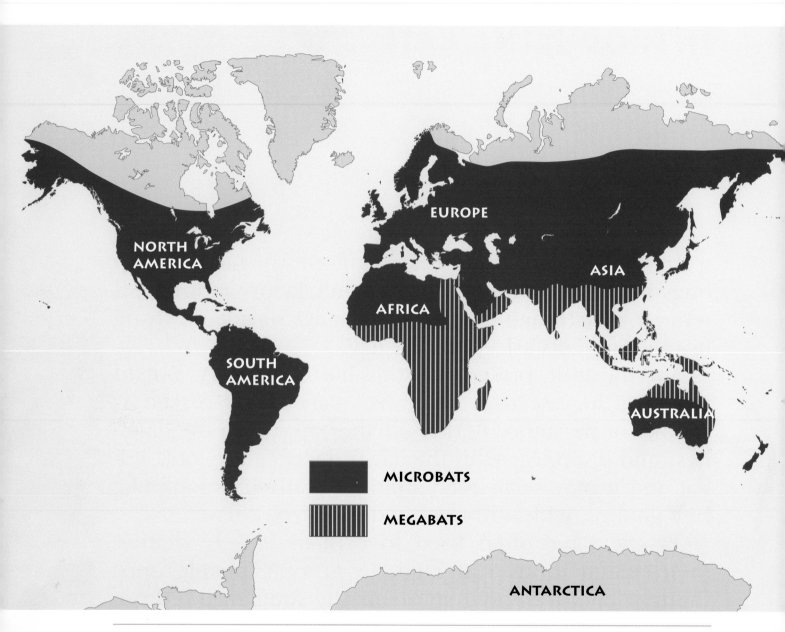

NORTH
AMERICA

SOUTH
AMERICA

EUROPE

AFRICA

ASIA

AUSTRALIA

ANTARCTICA

■ MICROBATS

||| MEGABATS

THIS MAP SHOWS WHERE BATS LIVE. BATS CAN BE FOUND ON ALL CONTINENTS
EXCEPT ANTARCTICA.

In the Caribbean islands, there is an old belief that bat blood can make you invisible or help you see in the dark. Even today, bats make many people think of horror stories like the legend of Count Dracula.

Some people see bats in a friendlier light. In one story told by the Cherokee Indians, a bat teams up with birds to win an animal ball game. In China, pictures of bats decorate cloth, pottery, and paper as symbols of good luck.

So are bats really blind? Do they really drink blood? And how do they sleep upside down?

The facts may surprise you. There are almost one thousand different *species*, or kinds, of bats. They live on every continent except Antarctica, and on many islands around the world. There are bats that sip nectar from flowers, like butterflies. Some nibble on fruit. There are ghost bats, bulldog bats, woolly bats, and wrinkle–faced bats, to name just a few. Each type has its own lifestyle. As you learn more about bats, you may be amazed at what they can do.

2
BAT BASICS

Bats are *mammals*, which means they belong to the same group of animals as horses, monkeys, dogs, and humans. Baby bats drink milk from their mother's breast, just as kittens do. They have soft fur on their bodies and are warm-blooded. Bats are typical mammals in some ways. But there is also something that sets them apart–they have wings.

Bats are the only mammals that can truly fly. The animals we call flying squirrels can only glide for short distances, using a flap of skin between their arms and legs like a parachute. But bats can fly with great skill and for many miles at a time.

The scientific name for bats is Chiroptera. It comes from the Greek words *cheiro*, which means hand, and *pteron*,

LARGE MOUSE-EARED BATS FLY CLOSE TO THE GROUND WHEN HUNTING. LIKE MANY BATS, THEY STEER WITH THE HELP OF A TAIL MEMBRANE—A FLAP OF SKIN THAT CONNECTS THEIR BACK LEGS AND ENCLOSES THEIR TAIL.

which means wing. In a way, the bat's hands are its wings. Each bat hand has four fingers and a thumb, like the hand of a person. The thumb is short and stubby, with a strong claw at the tip. But the fingers are very long and thin. A layer of skin stretches between them and connects to the sides of the bat's body and legs. This structure makes up the bat's wing.

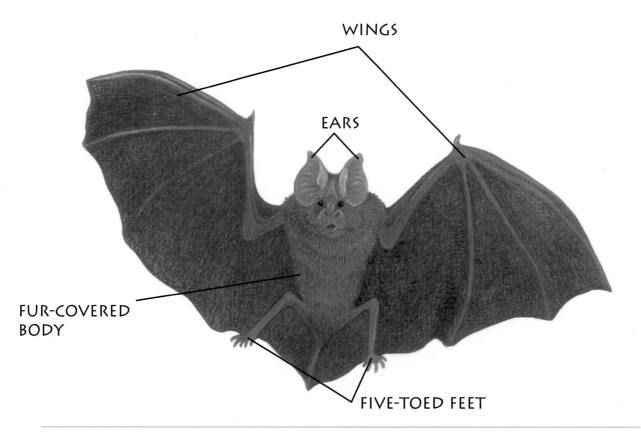

WINGS

EARS

FUR-COVERED BODY

FIVE-TOED FEET

THIS IS THE BODY OF A HORSESHOE BAT.

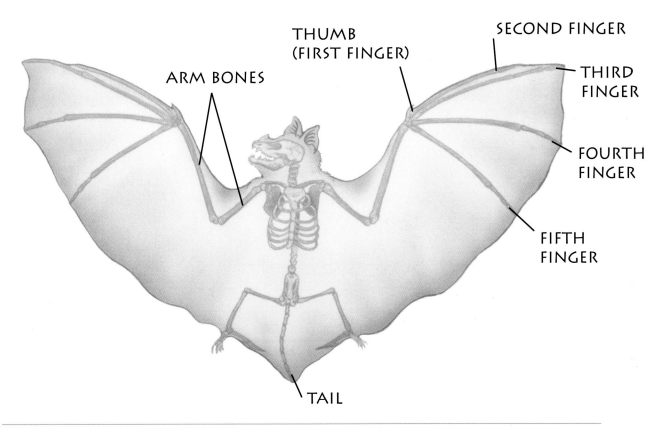

ARM BONES

THUMB
(FIRST FINGER)

SECOND FINGER

THIRD
FINGER

FOURTH
FINGER

FIFTH
FINGER

TAIL

THIS HORSESHOE BAT SKELETON SHOWS THE FIVE LONG FINGER BONES THAT SUPPORT THE WINGS.

A bat can fold its wings neatly, or open them up so the skin spreads tight like an open umbrella. When flying, it can change the shape of its wings to slow down, speed up, or shift direction. Some bats fly steadily and slowly. Others zoom, flutter, and zigzag while chasing their *prey*.

11

SEEING WITH SOUND

HOW DO MICROBATS FIND TINY BUGS IN THE DARK? THEY USE AN UNUSUAL SKILL CALLED *ECHOLOCATION*. WHEN MICROBATS FLY, THEY CALL OUT AGAIN AND AGAIN, MAKING PEEPS THAT LAST A SPLIT SECOND. AFTER EACH CRY, THEY LISTEN FOR ECHOES. AN ECHO MEANS THE SOUNDS ARE BOUNCING AGAINST AN OBJECT. A BAT CAN TELL FROM THE ECHOES HOW FAR AWAY AN OBJECT IS, ITS SIZE AND SHAPE, AND EVEN ITS TEXTURE.

MICROBATS SEE VERY WELL, BUT IN THE DARK THEIR ECHOLOCATION SKILLS ARE MUCH STRONGER THAN THEIR EYE-SIGHT. WITH ECHOLOCATION, THEY CAN "SEE" A WIRE AS FINE AS A HUMAN HAIR IN A PITCH-BLACK ROOM.

FOR ECHOLOCATION, BATS USE HIGH-FREQUENCY SOUNDS THAT PEOPLE CANNOT HEAR. BUT TO ANIMALS THAT DO HEAR THEM, THEY CAN BE VERY LOUD. IN FACT, SOME BATS HAVE TINY MUSCLES THAT PROTECT THEIR INNER EARS EACH TIME THEY CRY OUT, TO KEEP THEM FROM GOING DEAF FROM THE NOISE.

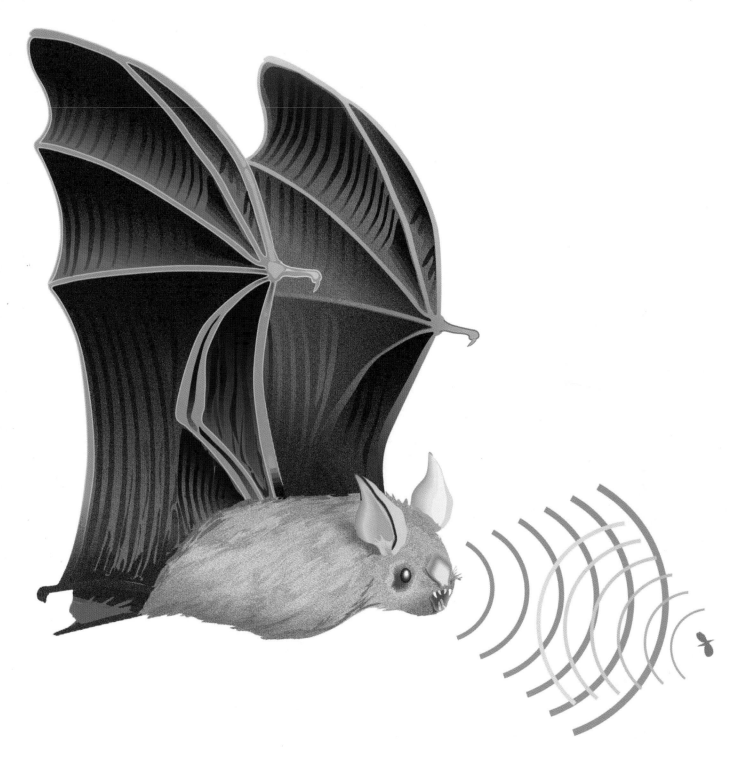

13

VAMPIRE BATS ARE SOCIAL ANIMALS. A LARGE GROUP WILL ROOST CLOSE TOGETHER AND SOMETIMES SHARE FOOD.

Most bats are *nocturnal*—that is, they are active only at night. At sunrise, they find a quiet place to perch. They grab hold of a branch, a leaf, or a ledge, and then sleep the day away, hanging upside down by their toes or claws.

A bat's legs are built to make hanging easy. The angle at which they are attached to the hip allows the knees to bend toward the back instead of the front. Strong, sharp claws help to grip surfaces. When a bat sleeps, it is perfectly relaxed, like a coat hanging from a hook.

Most bats like to *roost*, or hang, in a group. Many roost in trees, in caves, or under the roofs of buildings or bridges. A few have unusual hiding places. The disc-winged bats of Central and South America have tiny suction pads on their thumbs and feet that help them cling to smooth leaves. Generations of large mouse-tailed bats have roosted in the pyramids of Egypt for thousands of years.

3
CALLING ALL BATS

Scientists divide bats into two main groups: *megabats* and *microbats*. All megabats live in the tropical parts of Africa, Asia, and Australia, and on the islands of the southern Pacific Ocean. Microbats make their home in all parts of the world except the icy areas close to the North and South Poles.

Mega means big, and the megabat group includes the largest bats. Megabats have long, foxlike noses and large eyes. Because of their looks, many megabat species are called flying foxes. They depend on their keen sense of smell and sharp eyesight to find their way in the dark and track down food.

Megabats feed mostly on juicy tropical fruit and sweet-smelling flowers. A flying fox will travel miles to catch the scent of ripe bananas, figs, or mangoes. Then it will swoop down and carry off the fruit or eat it right away.

A MEGABAT HOLDS ON BY ITS THUMBS WHILE ENJOYING A MEAL.

BAT SPECIES

HERE ARE FIVE BAT SPECIES FROM AROUND THE WORLD.

Ghost bat
Wingspan: 20 inches (50 cm)
Head-to-tail length: 4-5 inches (10-12 cm)
Place of origin: Australia

Red bat
Wingspan: 13 inches (33 cm)
Head-to-tail length: 4-5 inches (10-12 cm)
Places of origin: North America, Central America, and northern South America

Tent-making bat
Wingspan: 8–9 inches (20-23 cm)
Head-to-tail length: 2 1/2 inches (6 cm)
Places of origin: Mexico, Central
America, and northern
South America

Vampire bat
Wingspan: 8 inches (20 cm)
Head-to-tail length: 3 inches (8 cm)
Places of origin: Mexico, Central
America, South America

Straw-colored fruit bat
Wingspan: 30 inches (76 cm)
Head-to-tail length: 6-8 inches (15-20 cm)
Place of origin: Africa

Some megabats drink flower nectar or eat *pollen*, a sticky powder the flower makes for reproduction. These bats often have tiny brushes on the ends of their tongues to help them collect food.

FRUIT BATS HAVE SHORT JAWS AND POWERFUL TEETH THAT HELP THEM TO PIERCE THE SKIN OF TOUGH FRUIT.

THIS LITTLE BROWN BAT CAUGHT A KATYDID BY "SEEING WITH SOUND."

Micro means small, and microbats tend to be smaller than megabats. All bats in North and South America belong to this group. They often have small eyes, big ears, and odd-looking noses. Most microbats eat insects, and they eat a lot of them. A typical microbat can munch more than two thousand bugs in a single night.

EACH FALL, MEXICAN FREE-TAIL BATS IN THE UNITED STATES FLY SOUTH TO FIND WARMER WEATHER AND FOOD. SOME MIGRATE AS FAR AS 800 MILES (1,287 KM).

SOME MICROBATS DRINK LIKE HUMMINGBIRDS. THIS LONG-TONGUED BAT IS SIPPING NECTAR FROM A BANANA FLOWER.

Some microbats prefer other food. A few species catch fish, others hunt frogs, and some feast on scorpions or spiders. Long–nosed bats dine on flower nectar and fruit, just like megabats. Vampire bats in Central and South America have the strangest diet. They make small cuts in the skin of an animal, then lap up the blood. Vampire bats may sound frightening, but their bite is painless, and they rarely touch humans. They draw blood mostly from farm animals, deer, and birds.

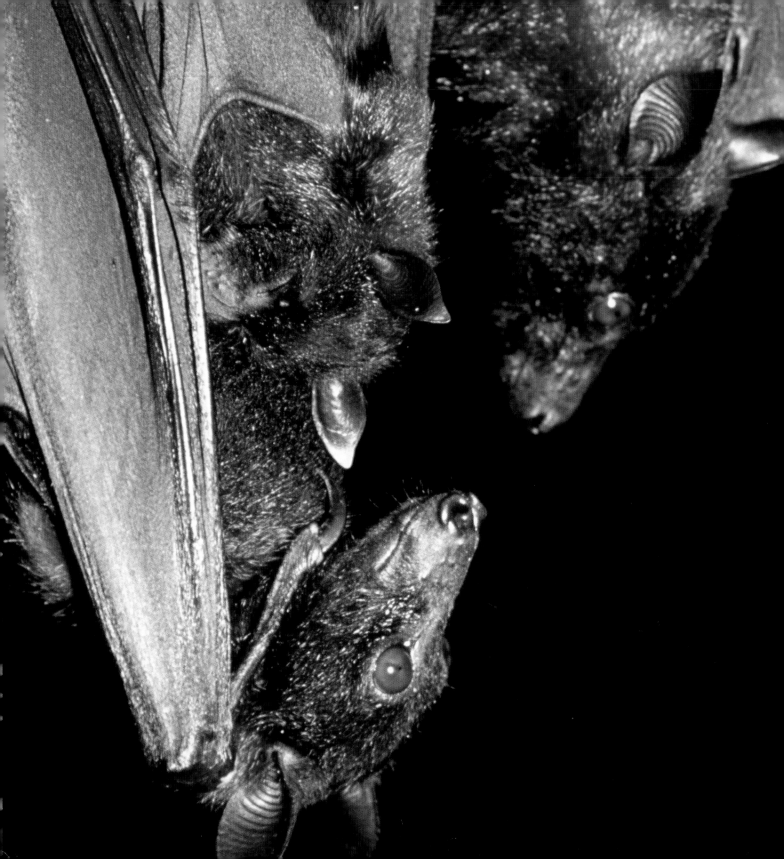

4
LIVING UPSIDE DOWN

Many bats start life in late spring, when the weather is warm and insects are buzzing. Mother bats usually give birth hanging upside down. The baby inches out of its mother's body and crawls along her belly to reach her nipples, which are tucked under her arms. While the baby nurses, the mother wraps her wings around it, keeping it safe and warm.

A female bat usually has just one baby, or *pup*, at a time. The mothers take care of their pups without help from the males. Flying foxes and many other bats take their pups along with them when they look for food. The pup uses its teeth and claws to cling to the fur of its mother's breast as she flies.

A MOTHER FRUIT BAT HOLDS ITS BABY CLOSE.

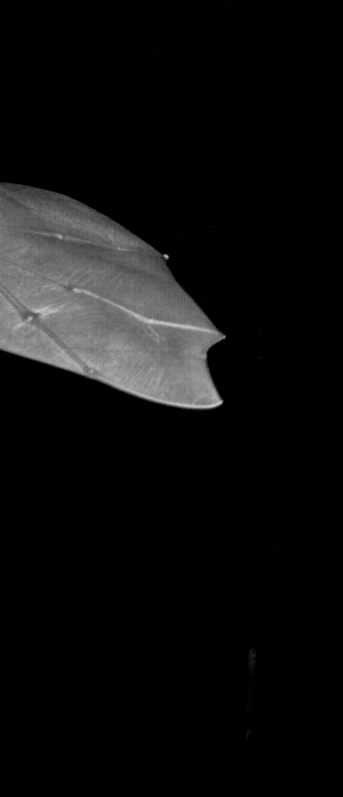

A MOTHER MEGABAT STAYS CLOSE
TO HER PUP UNTIL IT IS READY
TO FLY ON ITS OWN.

Mexican free-tail bats hunt alone, leaving their babies clinging to the ceiling of a warm cave when they are just a few hours old. When a mother returns, she goes back to the spot where she left her baby. A huge crowd of pups may be hanging there, and her own pup may be hard to see. But she calls out to it, sniffs the air for its scent, and listens for its cry. She soon finds it among all the others and tucks it under her wing to nurse.

Many bats start learning to fly when they are three or four weeks old. As they practice, an accident can be deadly. Bats that fall may be in trouble, because they are not built to take off easily from the ground.

Young bats usually roost near their mothers all summer. In many parts of the world, when autumn comes and the weather grows cooler, insects become harder to find. Around this time, some bat species *migrate* to warmer areas to get food. Many other bats *hibernate*. They spend the winter in a resting state, hanging in a cave or other sheltered place and living off the fat they have stored in their bodies.

When a bat hibernates, it does more than sleep. Its whole body slows down. The bat's body temperature drops

THESE FRUIT-EATING BATS CAN BE FOUND IN CAVES IN SOUTHEAST ASIA. THEY RAISE PUPS IN A GROUP CALLED A NURSING COLONY.

LITTLE BROWN BATS HIBERNATE DURING THE WINTER. IN THE CHILLY CAVE,
THEIR BODIES COOL DOWN AND GET COVERED WITH DROPLETS OF DEW.

to match the air around it. Its heart beats very slowly, and it only breathes about once every five minutes. This helps the bat save energy. Bats need a cool, protected place to slow down like this. They often leave their summer roost and stay in a cooler cave for the winter.

5
BATS AT RISK

Some bats can live to be thirty years old. Many others die young. In order to live to a ripe old age, a bat must watch out for *predators*. A snake can slither into a cave and nab a bat that is sleeping. An owl may lurk outside and catch a bat on the wing.

Bats also face danger from people. In some parts of Africa, Asia, and the Pacific Islands, people hunt and eat flying foxes. In Indonesia and Australia, farmers think of flying foxes as pests. Flying foxes do take some fruit from orchards, and fruit growers sometimes try to solve the problem by shooting the bats down.

But other types of bats can be helpful to farmers. Bats that drink nectar spread pollen as they move from one blossom to another. Plants need to be *pollinated* like

A GROUP OF ROOSTING INDIAN FLYING FOXES CAN FILL A LARGE TREE. SOME PEOPLE CONSIDER THESE BATS TO BE SACRED. OTHERS POISON THEM TO PROTECT THEIR CROPS, OR EVEN HUNT THEM FOR FOOD.

this in order to make fruit and seeds. Some plants, such as durian trees in Southeast Asia, bloom only at night. Their delicious fruit might never grow without bats that feed on the flowers.

THE LARGE-EARED HORSESHOE BAT IS RARE IN AUSTRALIA. PEOPLE HAVE HARMED IT WITHOUT MEANING TO, BY CLOSING OLD MINES WHERE IT MAKES ITS HOME.

Microbats help protect crops by eating insects. They catch beetles, moths, and leafhoppers that can ruin farmers' fields. One group of Mexican free-tail bats in central Texas catches about a hundred tons of insects each night. Imagine how many bugs there would be if the bats disappeared!

A BACKYARD BAT HOUSE GIVES BATS A PLACE TO LIVE. THE VISITING BATS WILL HELP OUT BY PROVIDING NATURAL PEST CONTROL—ONE BAT CAN EAT OVER SIX HUNDRED MOSQUITOES IN AN HOUR!

FLYING FOXES IN INDONESIA.
THESE BATS HELP BY SPREADING
SEEDS FROM THE FRUITS THEY EAT
SO NEW PLANTS WILL GROW.

A HARP TRAP DEMONSTRATION—THESE TRAPS ARE OFTEN USED BY BAT RESEARCHERS. HARP-LIKE STRINGS CATCH BATS IN FLIGHT WITHOUT TANGLING THEIR WINGS. THEN THE BAT GENTLY DROPS INTO THE CANVAS BAG BELOW.

Many bats are disappearing. Around the world, the bat population is shrinking. One reason is that people harm their *habitats*–the places where they live and find food. When farmers use pesticides to kill insects, bats can swallow the poison along with their prey. People can also hurt bats by entering caves where they raise pups or hibernate. If bats wake up during the winter, they use up energy. They can lose the fat they need to survive until spring.

Today, many people are working to help bats. Some caves now have gates that let bats fly in and out but keep people away. Many families even build bat houses to offer a roosting place near their home. We still have a lot to learn about bats and their amazing abilities. The more we know, the better we can help them survive.

Chiroptera: The scientific name for bats, which means hand–wing.

echolocation: The ability to locate objects by calling out and listening for echoes.

hibernate: To spend the winter in a resting state that appears similar to a deep sleep.

high–frequency sounds: Sounds that are too high for humans to hear.

mammals: Animals that have hair on their bodies, give birth to live young, and nurse their young with their own milk.

megabats: Bats with large eyes and foxlike noses that feed on flowers or fruit in Africa, Asia, Australia, and the South Pacific.

microbats: Bats with small eyes and large ears that live in most parts of the world; most feed on insects.

migrate: To travel from one area to another, usually when seasons change.

nocturnal: To be active at night.

pollen: A powder that must spread from one flower to another before a plant can make fruit and seeds.

pollinate: Spread pollen from one flower to another.

predators: Animals that hunt other animals.

prey: An animal that is hunted by other animals.

roost: To rest in one place, often in trees, caves, or under the roofs of buildings.

species: A particular type of living thing.

FIND OUT MORE

BOOKS

Ackerman, Diane. *Bats: Shadows in the Night.* New York: Alfred A. Knopf Books for Young Readers, 1997.

Arnold, Caroline. *Bat.* New York: Morrow Junior Books, 1996.

Gibbons, Gail. *Bats.* New York: Holiday House, 1999.

Halton, Cheryl Mays. *Those Amazing Bats.* Minneapolis: Dillon Press, 1991.

Merrick, Patrick. *Vampire Bats.* Chanhassen, MN: Child's World, 2000.

Pringle, Laurence. *Bats! Strange and Wonderful.* Honesdale, PA: Boyds Mills Press, 2000.

Stuart, Dee. *Bats: Mysterious Flyers of the Night.* Minneapolis: Carolrhoda Books, 1994.

Wilson, Don E. *Bats in Question: The Smithsonian Answer Book.* Washington, D.C.: Smithsonian Institution Press, 1997.

WEB SITES

Bat Conservation International
www.batcon.org

Bats4Kids
http://members.aol.com/bats4kids/

ABOUT THE AUTHOR

Margaret Dornfeld is the author of several books for young people, including *Wisconsin* and *Vermont* in the Marshall Cavendish Celebrate the States series.

INDEX

Page numbers for illustrations are in **boldface.**

maps, 6

babies. See pups
birth, 27
body, **10**

caves, 30, **31, 32**, 33, 41
Central America, 15, 25
claws, 10, 15
communication, 30
conservation, **37, 40,**
    41, 44

days and nights, **4**, 5, 15
disc-winged bats, 15

ears, **10**, 12, 21, **36**
eating, 7, **14, 16**, 17, **20,**
    21, 24, 25
echolocation, 12, **13, 21**
ecology, 35–41, **38–39**
Egypt, 15
endangerment, **36**, 41
eyes, 17, 21

farmers, 35–41, **38–39**
feet, **10**, 15
females, 27–30, **28–29**
flying, 9, 11, 30
flying foxes, 17, 27, **34,**
    35, **38–39**
food, 7, 17–25, 30, 35, 37

bats as, 35
    poisoned, 41
    for pups, 27
fruit bats, 19, **19, 20,**
    26, 31, 35
fur, 9

geographic distribution,
    6, 7, 15, 17–19, 21
ghost bats, 18, **18**

habitat loss, **36**, 41
hands and fingers, 9–10,
    10, 11, 15
hanging, 15
hibernation, 30–33, **32**
    interruption of, 41
hiding places, 15
horseshoe bats, **4, 11,**
    36
hunting
    by bats, 11–12, 17, **21**
    of bats, 35

jaws, **20**

legends, 5–7
legs, 15
life span, 35
little brown bats, 5, **21,**
    32
long-nosed bats, 25

long-tongued bats, **24**

males, 27
mammals, 9
megabats, **16**, 17–20, **18,**
    19, 21, 28–29, 35–36
Mexican free-tailed bats,
    22–23, 30, **37**
microbats, 12, 17, 19, **19,**
    21, 21–25, **24**
migrations, **22–23**, 30
mouse-eared bats, **9**
mouse-tailed bats, 15

name, 9–10
nests. See caves; roosts
North America, 21,
    22–23, 37
nose, 17, 21
nursing colonies, 30, **31**

parenting, 27–30,
    28–29, 31
pesticides, 41
pollen, 20
    spreading, 35–36,
    38–39
predators, 35
pups, **26**, 27–30,
    28–29, 31

red bats, 18, **18**

roosts, 15, 30, 33, **34,**
    37, 41

sizes, 17–19
skeleton, **11**
sleeping, 15
    See also hibernation
smell, sense of, 17, 30
social interaction, **14,**
    15, **22–23**
sounds, 12, **13**
South America, 15, 21, 25
species, **18**, 18–19, **19**
    number of, 7
straw-colored fruit bat,
    19, **19**

tail, **11**
tail membrane, **8**
tails, **9**
teeth, **20**
tent-making bat, 19, **19**
toes, **10**, 15
tongue, 20, **24**
traps, **40**

vampire bats, **14**, 19,
    19, 25
vision, 12, 17, **21**

Web sites, 44
wings, 9–11, **10, 11**

OXFORD FREE LIBRARY
339 Main Street
Oxford, Ma. 01540